Hal Leonard Student Piano Library

Piano Theory Workbook

Book 5

Authors
**Barbara Kreader, Fred Kern,
Phillip Keveren, Mona Rejino,
Karen Harrington**

Editor
Carol Klose

Illustrator
Fred Bell

FOREWORD

The **Piano Theory Workbooks** present theory writing assignments that coordinate page-by-page with the **Piano Lessons** books in the **Hal Leonard Student Piano Library**.

Creative activities introduce the language of music and its symbols for sound, silence and rhythm. Ear training exercises and basic theory help students learn to write and play the music they are learning as well as the music they create themselves.

Best wishes,

Barbara Kreader   Fred Kern   Phillip Keveren

Mona Rejino   Karen Harrington

ISBN 978-0-634-01482-6

Visit Hal Leonard Online at
www.halleonard.com

World headquarters, contact:
Hal Leonard
7777 West Bluemound Road
Milwaukee, WI 53213
Email: info@halleonard.com

In Europe, contact:
Hal Leonard Europe Limited
1 Red Place
London, W1K 6PL
Email: info@halleonardeurope.com

In Australia, contact:
Hal Leonard Australia Pty. Ltd.
4 Lentara Court
Cheltenham, Victoria, 3192 Australia
Email: info@halleonard.com.au

Two for Six
Compound Time

$\frac{6}{8}$ meter is **compound time**. Each ♩. divides into ♪♪♪ . Feel and count the pulse as:

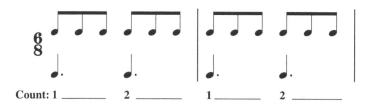

Count: 1 _____ 2 _____ | 1 _____ 2 _____

1. In this example from *The Windmill*, count the pulses by writing "1 - 2 - " in the blanks in each measure.

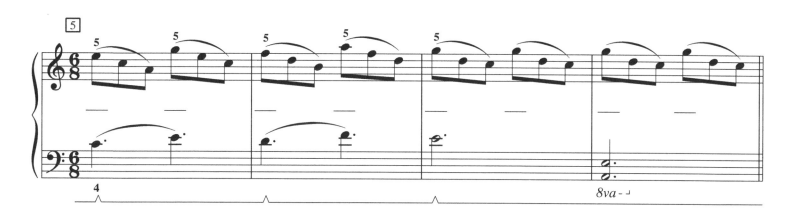

2. When counting $\frac{6}{8}$ meter with two pulses to a measure:

   How many eighth notes fill one pulse? _____

   How many eighth notes fill one measure? _____

   What kind of note lasts for one pulse? _____

   What kind of note lasts for two pulses? _____

3. Play the excerpt above, counting "1 - 2 - " in each measure.

Pedaling Has Its Ups and Downs

1. Play this piece without pedal.
2. Write in the pedal markings. Trace the blue line and indicate a pedal change
   at the beginning of each measure by adding ∧ under each bass-clef whole note.
3. Play the piece with pedal.

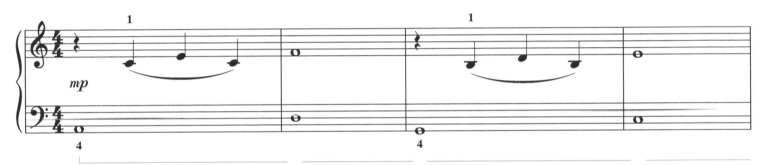

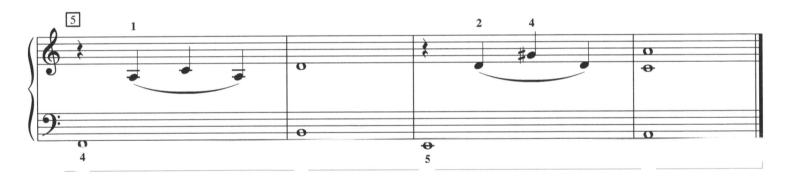

1. Play this piece without pedal.
2. Play the piece again, adding pedal. Use your ear to decide where to change it.
3. Write in the pedal markings.

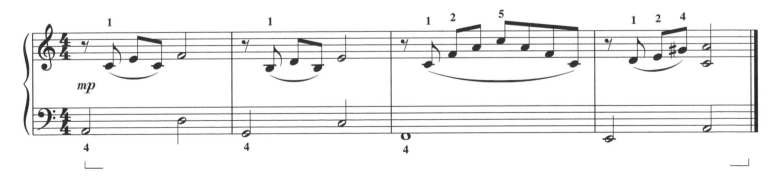

3

The Score Is Four to One

Sixteenth Notes

Four sixteenth notes fill the time of _____ quarter note(s) or _____ eighth notes.

1. Finish writing the counts beneath the right-hand notes in the example below.
2. Play the example, which is in A Minor.

3. Complete the following example by transposing the A Minor melody to its related major, C.
4. Play your transposition.

Extra for Experts

Transpose the two examples above by playing them in:
    D Minor/F Major
    E Minor/G Major

Relay Hand-Off

1. Write the correct Roman numeral in the blank below each chord.
2. Write the correct letter symbol in the blank above each chord.
3. Play *Relay Hand-Off*.

4. Using the above example as a guide, transpose *Relay Hand-Off* to C Major and A Minor by writing in the missing chords, melody, Roman numerals, and letter symbols.
5. Play your transposition.

6. Transpose *Relay Hand-Off* to F Major and D Minor by writing in the missing chords and melody.
7. Play your transposition.

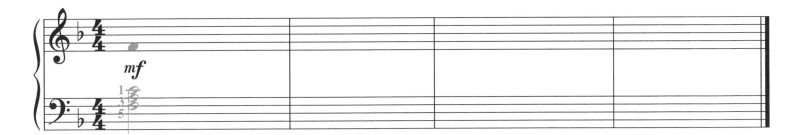

Extra for Experts
Play all three versions of *Relay Hand-Off* one after the other, without pausing.
Notice that both hands move down a 3rd for each new key.

Use with Lesson Book 5, pgs. 6-7

Moving On Up
in F Major

The Primary Chords in **F Major** are:

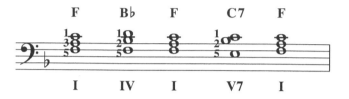

1. Add the F Major key signature to each grand staff below.
2. Write the missing scale fingering in the blue boxes.
3. Using the Roman numerals and the letter symbols as a guide,
   write the primary chords in close position.
4. Play each example.

Extra for Experts

Transpose the above examples to the key of G Major, using the correct fingering for the G Major scale.

Moving On Up
in D Minor

The Primary Chords in **D Minor** are:

Dm	Gm	Dm	A7	Dm
i	iv	i	V7	i

1. Add the D Minor key signature to each grand staff below.
2. Change the D Natural Minor Scale to D Harmonic Minor
   by writing a sharp sign in front of the 7th degree of each scale.
3. Write the missing scale fingering in the blue boxes.
4. Identify the primary chords by writing Roman numerals in the blanks, and letter symbols in the pink boxes.
5. Play each example.

Extra for Experts
Transpose the above examples to the key of E Minor, using the correct fingering for the E Minor scale.

Use with Lesson Book 5, pg. 9

Making a Repeat Appearance!

MOTIVE

A **Motive** is a short melodic pattern of notes that reappears throughout a piece.

SEQUENCE

A **Sequence** is the repetition of the same rhythmic and intervallic pattern at a different pitch.

1. Continue the two-measure **motive** as a **sequence** throughout this phrase using only notes from the C Major scale.

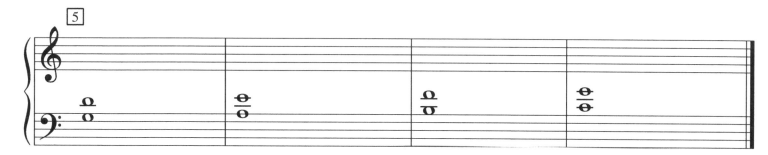

2. Write the following **sequence** by continuing the two-measure **motive**.

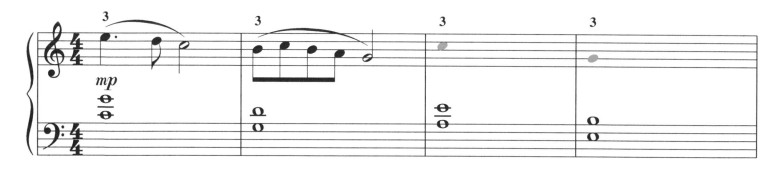

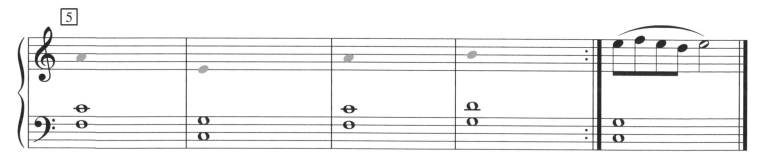

Extra for Experts
Play each example above.

Sixteenth Rests

SIXTEENTH REST

A **Sixteenth Rest** fills the time of one sixteenth note.

Dividing quarter notes into sub-beats makes it easier to hear the rhythm of sixteenth notes and rests. Say the beats as you clap or tap the rhythms below.

Easy As Pie

1. Using "1 - &" or syllables your teacher suggests, write the beats under the notes and rests in the blue areas below.
2. Say the beats as you tap or clap the rhythm.
3. Say the words to *Easy As Pie* in rhythm.

Huck - le - ber - ry, blue - ber - ry, straw - ber - ry pie,   Bake 'em up!   Bake 'em up!   Give it a try!

Give 'em to your mo - ther,   or to your sis - ter,   or to your bro - ther,   or else to me!

Extra for Experts

Set your metronome as follows and say the words to *Easy As Pie* in rhythm.

♩ = 60   ♩ = 72   ♩ = 80

Use with Lesson Book 5, pg. 11

Where Is the Rest of It?

1. In each piece of pie, add the rest to complete each one-measure rhythm.
2. As your teacher claps each rhythm below, point to the piece of pie that matches it.

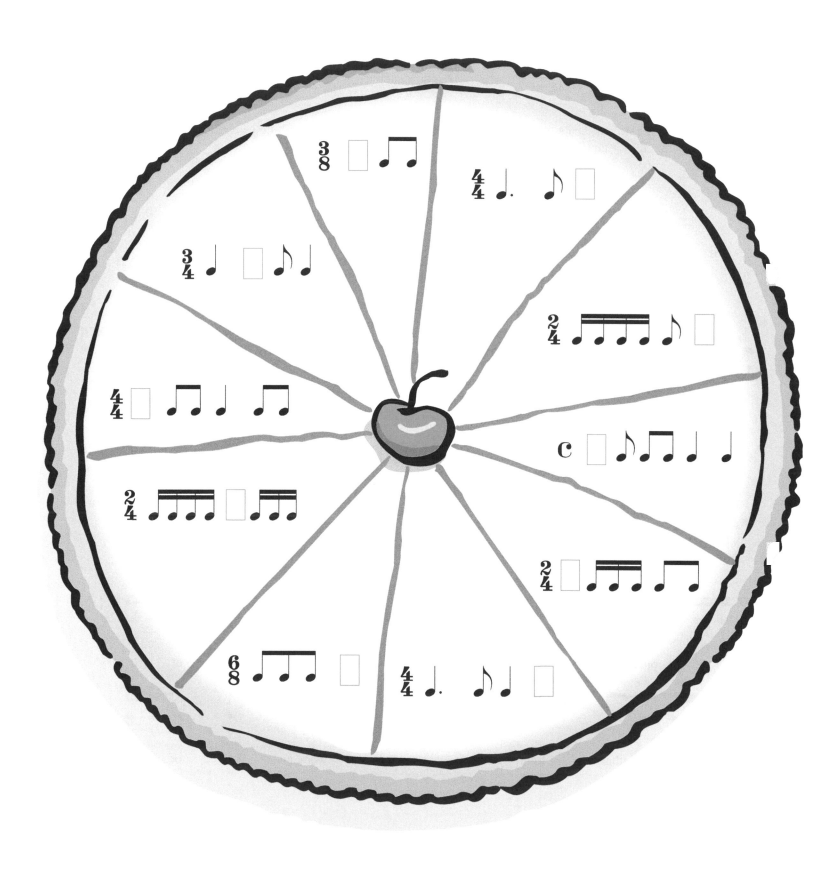

The 𝅘𝅥𝅮𝅘𝅥𝅮𝅘𝅥 and 𝅘𝅥𝅮𝅘𝅥𝅮𝅘𝅥 Rhythm Patterns

At the Aquarium

1. Using "1 - &" or syllables your teacher suggests, write the beats under the notes and rests in the blue areas.
2. Say the beats as you tap or clap the rhythm.
3. Say the words to *At the Aquarium* in rhythm.

Sea   li-ons,   jel - ly - fish,   man-ta rays   too,   Fly - ing fish,   oc - to - pus,   look   back   at   you!

Don't Tell!

The rhythm pattern below is from a famous overture.

1. Circle all the 𝅘𝅥𝅮𝅘𝅥𝅮𝅘𝅥 rhythm patterns you find.
2. Tap or clap the rhythm, counting aloud.
   What is the name of this famous piece?

Answer: *William Tell Overture* by Rossini

11

The Incredible Stretching and Shrinking Chords

M - aug - m - dim

Triads can have four different sounds or qualities:

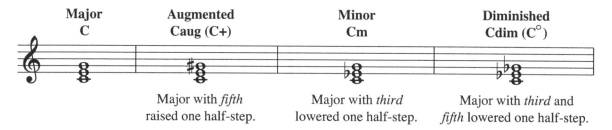

Major	Augmented	Minor	Diminished
C	Caug (C+)	Cm	Cdim (C°)
	Major with *fifth* raised one half-step.	Major with *third* lowered one half-step.	Major with *third* and *fifth* lowered one half-step.

1. Accidentals are missing from some of the triads below.
   Use sharps or flats to make the necessary corrections.
2. Play the chord progression.

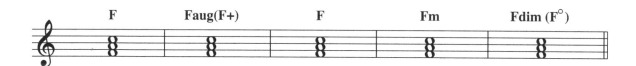

F   Faug(F+)   F   Fm   Fdim (F°)

3. Write the correct letter symbol in the blank above each triad.
4. Play the chord progression.

G

5. Your teacher will play six different triads. Identify the quality of each one by circling the correct chord symbol.

| 1. | **M** | **m** | 3. | **aug** | **dim** | 5. | **M** | **aug** | **dim** |
| 2. | **M** | **m** | 4. | **aug** | **dim** | 6. | **M** | **m** | **dim** |

Chords of the Key

PRIMARY TRIADS

Chords built on the 1st, 4th, and 5th tones of the major scale are called **Primary Triads**.

These triads are **major** and use *upper case* Roman numerals **I - IV - V**.

SECONDARY TRIADS

Chords built on the 2nd, 3rd, and 6th tones of the major scale are called **Secondary Triads**.

These triads are **minor** and use *lower case* Roman numerals **ii - iii - vi**.

DIMINISHED TRIAD

The chord built on the 7th tone of the major scale is **diminished** (vii°).

Roman numerals indicate each chord's root and its scale degree.
Using *only* notes from the **C Major Scale**:

1. Write the correct **primary** triads in the green squares.
2. Write the correct **secondary** triads in the yellow circles.
3. Write a **diminished** triad in the red triangle.

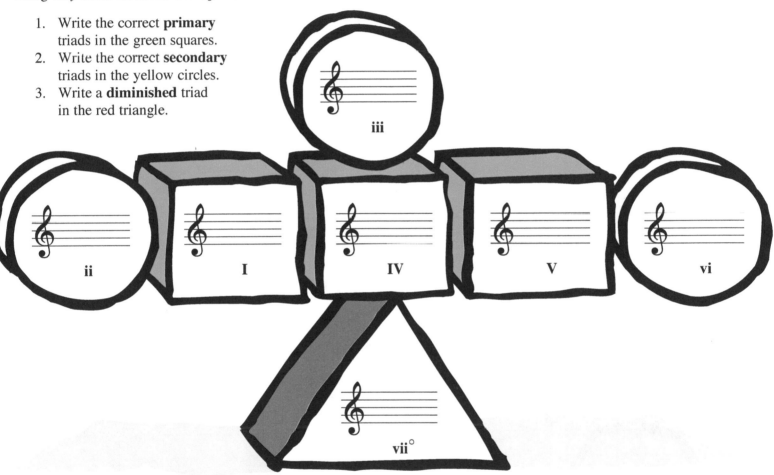

The triads below are in the key of C Major.

1. Write the correct Roman numeral in each blank.
2. Write the correct letter symbol in each blue box.
3. Play each triad.

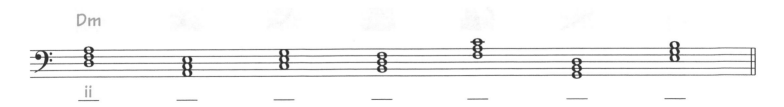

Use with Lesson Book 5, pg. 17

Juggling Triads

1. Build a root position triad on each scale degree in the key of G Major.
2. Write the Roman numeral in each blank.
3. Write the letter symbol in each blue box.
4. Play each triad.

Using *only* notes from the **G Major Scale**:

1. Write three different **primary** triads in the green circles.
2. Write three different **secondary** triads in the yellow circles.
3. Write a **diminished** triad in the red circle.

Triads Encore

1. In each blue box, write the missing letter symbol, Roman numeral, or root position triad in the key of F Major.
2. Play each triad.

Using *only* notes from the **F Major Scale**:

   1. Write three different **primary** triads in the green circles.
   2. Write three different **secondary** triads in the yellow circles.
   3. Write a **diminished** triad in the red circle.

Use with Lesson Book 5, pg. 17

Season Opener – Major League Triads

A chord is in **open position** when the *third* is moved an octave higher from root position.

1. On the grand staff below, change the C Major root position triads to **open position** by moving the *third* of each triad one octave higher.
2. Label the chords of the key in C Major by writing the Roman numerals in the blanks below the staff.
3. Play each chord.

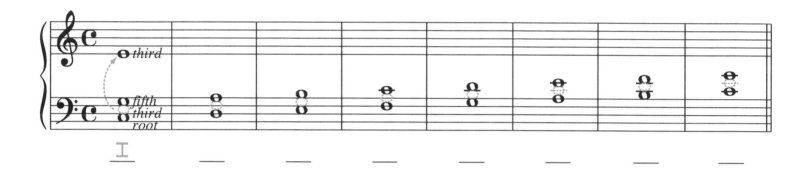

4. Identify the root position and open position triads in this excerpt from *Curtain Call* by writing the correct Roman numerals in the blanks.
5. Play the excerpt.

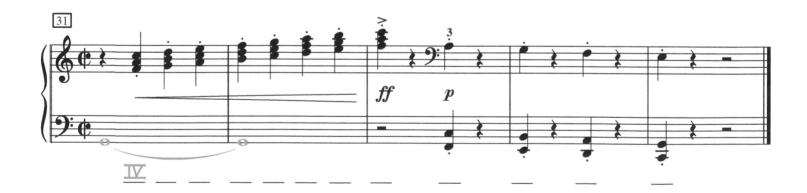

Use with Lesson Book 5, pgs. 17-19

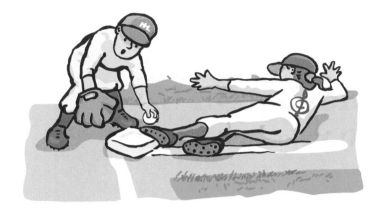

Treble Clef Steals Third
Building Open Position Triads

1. On the grand staff below, write open position triads from the given root in the key of F Major.
2. Write the Roman numerals in the blanks.
3. Write the letter symbols in the blue boxes.
4. Play each chord.

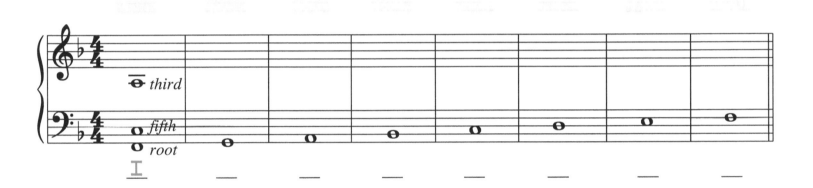

This practice version of *The Clown* by Rebikov uses open position triads in the key of F Major.

1. Identify these triads by writing Roman numerals in the blanks.
2. Play the example.

Use with Lesson Book 5, pgs. 20-21

Moving On Up
in D Major and B Minor

1. Add the D Major key signature to the grand staff below.
2. Complete the D Major Scale using the finger numbers as a guide.
3. Identify the primary chords in close position by writing Roman numerals in the blue boxes.
4. Play the example.

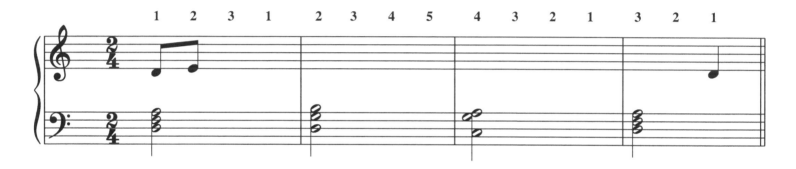

1. Add the B Minor key signature to the grand staff below.
2. Change the B Natural Minor Scale to B Harmonic Minor by writing a sharp sign in front of the 7th degree of the scale.
3. Write the missing scale fingering in the blue boxes.
4. Using the Roman numerals as a guide, write the primary chords in close position.
5. Play the example.

Extra for Experts
Transpose the two examples above to each pair of keys below.
    C Major/A Minor
    F Major/D Minor
    G Major/ E Minor

Use with Lesson Book 5, pgs. 22-23

Match Game

1. Match each scale below to its correct fingering by writing **A**, **B**, **C**, or **D** in the blue box.

      A. 5 4 3 2 1 3 2 1   **C.** 4 3 2 1 4 3 2 1

      B. 1 2 3 4 1 2 3 4   **D.** 1 2 3 1 2 3 4 5

 = R.H.   = L.H.

_____

_____

_____

_____

_____

_____

2. Identify each scale above as Major, Natural Minor, or Harmonic Minor by writing its name in the blank beside it.

3. Listen as your teacher plays six scales. Identify each one as Major, Natural Minor, or Harmonic Minor. Write your answers below.

1. _____   4. _____

2. _____   5. _____

3. _____   6. _____

Teacher's Examples on pg. 39

Use with Lesson Book 5, pgs. 22-23

Questions and Answers

Musical phrases often occur in pairs.
When the first phrase is called the **question**, the second phrase is called the **answer**.

Parallel answers begin with the same pitches and include an almost identical ending.

Contrasting answers include musical material different from the question.

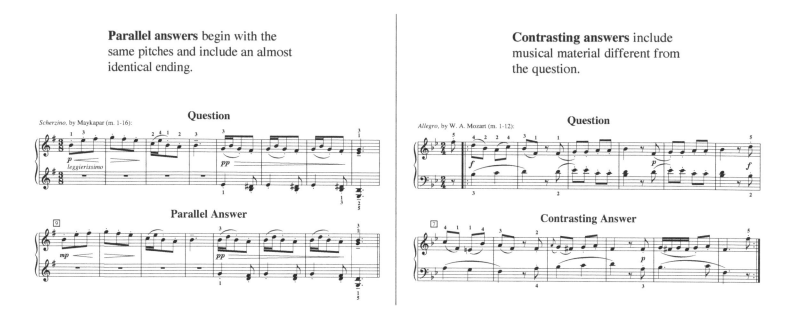

1. Write a **parallel** answer, using only the notes in the C Major scale.

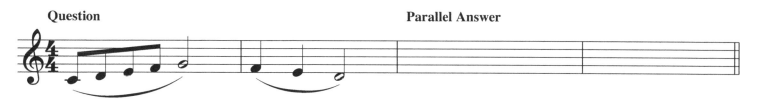

2. Write a **contrasting** answer, using only the notes in the D Minor scale.

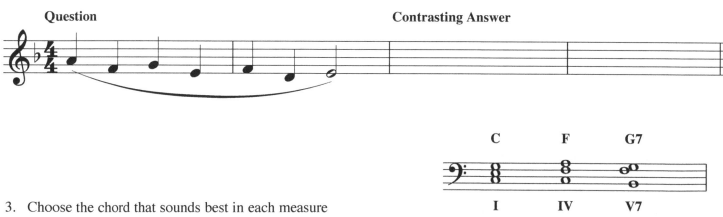

3. Choose the chord that sounds best in each measure and write it in the blue box.

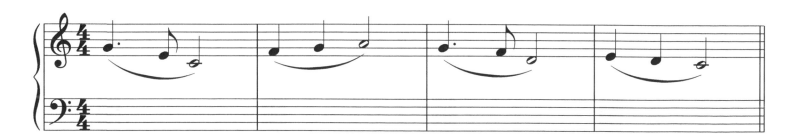

Name That Tune!

**DOTTED EIGHTH-
SIXTEENTH NOTE
PATTERN**

1. Complete each rhythmic example below by adding either bar lines or a time signature.

_____

_____

_____

_____

2. Each rhythm above matches one of the following melodies. Listen as your teacher plays each one.
   Write the title of the song in the blank beside the rhythm that matches it.

   • **Ode to Joy**   • **Alouette**

   • **Simple Gifts**   • **The Star Spangled Banner**

Teacher's Examples on pg. 39

Use with Lesson Book 5, pg. 25

The Dotted-Rhythm Website

www. ♩. ♪ ♩ ♩ ♩. ♩ .com

Complete each measure by drawing the correct dotted-rhythm pattern from the title above in each blue box.

Extra for Experts
Set your metronome on mm ♩ = 72 and clap each rhythm pattern.

Breaking Up is *Not* Hard to Do
Subdividing Quarter Notes

Tap and count the following rhythm:

Listen carefully as your teacher claps either the rhythm in Column **A** or the rhythm in Column **B**.
Circle the rhythm that matches the example your teacher claps.

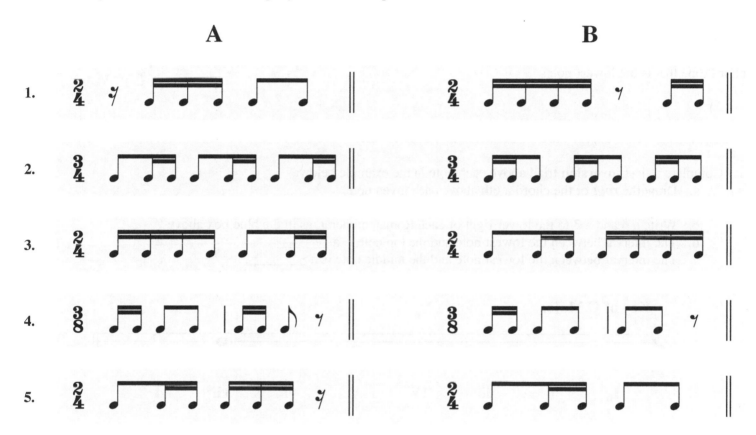

The musical examples below should match the rhythms you circled.
Match each example to its correct rhythmic notation by writing 1, 2, 3, 4, or 5 in the blue boxes.

23

Teacher's Examples on pg. 39

Use with Lesson Book 5, pg. 28

Triad Turnovers
Root Position and First Inversion Triads

A triad can have more than one position:

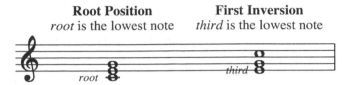

Roman numerals indicate each chord's root and its scale degree. When a chord is inverted, the lowest note changes but the letter names of the three chord tones remain the same. **Inversions** are identified by the chord tone that is the lowest note.

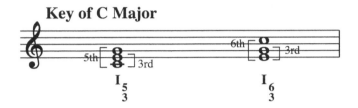

In a **first inversion** triad, the *third* of the chord is the lowest note.

1. Complete a **first inversion** triad above each note in the example below.
    a. Draw the *root* of the chord a 6th above each given note.
    b. Complete each triad by drawing the *fifth* of the chord a 3rd above each given note.
    c. Write a **6** and a **3** to the lower right of each Roman numeral, as in the blue box above.*
    d. The interval between the lowest note and the top note is a _____.
        The interval between the lowest note and the middle note is a _____.

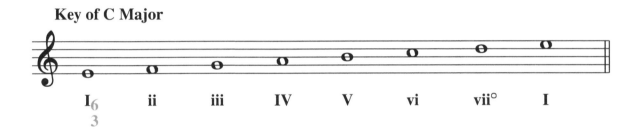

2. Identify the *root*, *third*, or *fifth* of the chord in each first inversion triad below.

* In **first inversion** chords, the number 3 indicating the interval of a 3rd is generally omitted, and the chord symbol is often abbreviated: I₆, ii₆, etc.

Triad Turnovers – Seconds Please!
Root Position, First and Second Inversion Triads

A triad can have three positions:

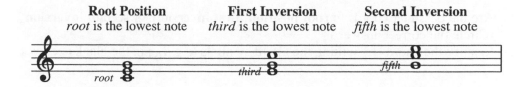

Roman numerals indicate each chord's root and its scale degree. When a chord is inverted, the lowest note changes but the letter names of the three chord tones remain the same. **Inversions** are identified by the chord tone that is the lowest note.

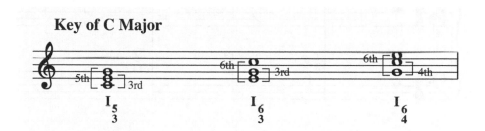

In a **second inversion** triad, the *fifth* of the chord is the lowest note.

1. Complete a **second inversion** triad above each note in the example below.
   a. Draw the *third* of the chord a 6th above each given note.
   b. Complete each triad by drawing the *root* of the chord a 4th above each given note.
   c. Write a **6** and a **4** to the lower right of each Roman numeral, as in the blue box above.
   d. The interval between the lowest note and the top note is a _____.
   The interval between the lowest note and the middle note is a _____.

Key of C Major

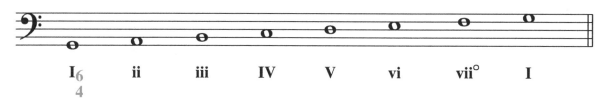

2. Identify the *root*, *third*, or *fifth* of the chord in each second inversion triad below.

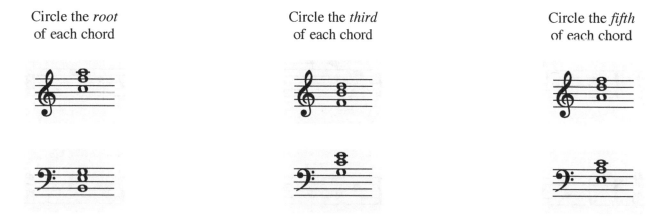

Use with Lesson Book 5, pg. 31

Inversion Diversion

The following excerpt is in the key of C Major.

1. Are the bass-clef chords in **root position**, **first inversion**, or **second inversion**?
   (Circle the correct answer.)
2. Identify the chords by writing the chord symbols (e.g. I₆) in the blanks below the staff.

Michael, Row The Boat Ashore

— — —

Listening for Chord Positions

Your teacher will play the musical example in Column **A**, **B**, or **C**. Circle the chord that matches the one your teacher plays.

The following excerpt is in the key of A Minor.

1. Are the chords in measures 3 and 5 in **root position**, **first inversion**, or **second inversion**?
    (Circle the correct answer.)
2. In measures 1 and 3, write the correct chord symbols in the blanks below the chords.
3. Identify the chords in measures 1, 3, 4 and 5 by writing the correct letter symbols in the blue boxes.

Arabesque, by Burgmüller

The following excerpt is in the key of C Major.

1. Are the treble-clef chords in **root position**, **first inversion**, or **second inversion**?
    (Circle the correct answer.)
2. Identify each chord by writing the correct letter symbols in the blue boxes.

Bouncing Back, by Keveren

Use with Lesson Book 5, pg. 31

Moving On Up
in B♭ Major and G Minor

1. Add the B♭ Major key signature to the grand staff below.
2. Write the missing scale fingering in the blue boxes below each scale degree.
3. Using the letter symbols as a guide, write the primary chords in close position.
4. Play the example.

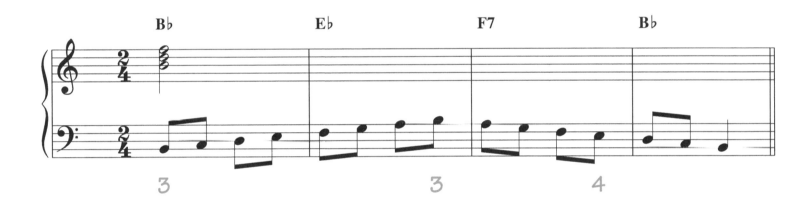

1. Add the G Minor key signature to the grand staff below.
2. Complete the G Natural Minor Scale, using the finger numbers as a guide.
3. Change the G Natural Minor Scale to G Harmonic Minor by writing a sharp sign in front of the 7th degree of each scale.
4. Identify the primary chords in close position by writing the Roman numerals in the blue boxes.
5. Play the example.

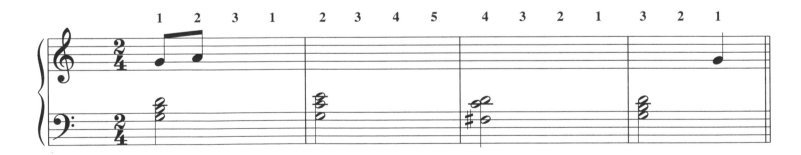

Use with Lesson Book 5, pgs. 36-37

Now Try This!

1. Match each scale below to its correct fingering by writing **A**, **B**, **C** or **D** in the blue box.

    A. 3 2 1 4 3 2 1 3   **C.** 2 1 2 3 1 2 3 4
                                                       (4)

    B. 5 4 3 2 1 3 2 1   **D.** 1 2 3 1 2 3 4 5

    𝄞 = R.H.   𝄢 = L.H.

_____

_____

_____

_____

2. Identify each scale above as Major, Natural Minor, or Harmonic Minor by writing its name in the blank beside it.

3. One chord is missing from each chord progression below. Listen as your teacher plays the complete progression and write the Roman numerals for the missing chords in the blue boxes. Choose from I (i), IV (iv), or V7.

    1.   I   IV   I   **4.**   I   V7   I   I

    2.   I   V7   I   **5.**   i   V7   i

    3.   i   iv   i   **6.**   iv   V7   i

Teacher's Examples on pg. 40

Use with Lesson Book 5, pgs. 36-37

Improvising in ABA Form

1. To create the **A section** of your improvisation, play the following question phrase.
   Improvise various answers (parallel and contrasting), using notes from the C Major scale.
   Notate your favorite answer.

2. To create the **B section**, play various sequences of the following motive using notes
   from the A Harmonic Minor scale. Notate your favorite version.

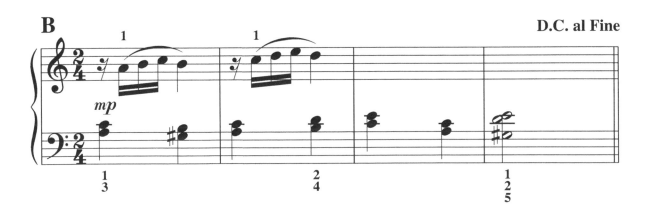

3. Combine the two lines and play your A B A composition.

Chromatic Construction

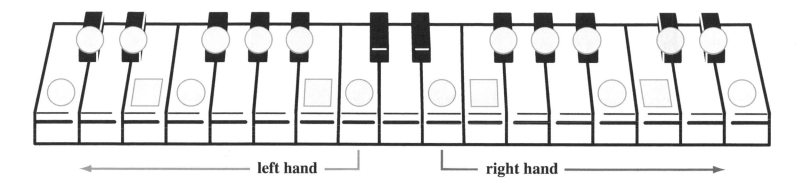

A **Chromatic Scale** is formed by playing half steps up and down the keyboard. To discover the best fingering for each hand, complete the following steps and write the fingering on the keyboard above.

1. Write a "3" in each circle on the black keys.
   Play each black key with the third finger of each hand.
2. Write a "2" in each blue **box** and a "1" in each blue **circle** on the keyboard.
3. Notice each pair of white keys marked "1" and "2." These are the only chromatic half steps made up of two white keys.

   With your right hand, play each pair of white keys together, moving **up and down** the keyboard.

   With your left hand, play each pair of white keys together, moving **down and up** the keyboard.

4. Write a "1" on all remaining white keys.
5. Play the complete chromatic scale using the fingering you have written.

   Right hand: Start on E, going **up and down** the keyboard.

   Left hand: Start on C, going **down and up** the keyboard.

Extra for Experts
Play both hands together in contrary motion.

31

Use with Lesson Book 5, pg. 42

Chromatic Inspection

When a **chromatic scale** is written on the staff, sharps are normally used in the *ascending* scale and flats are used in the *descending* scale.

The following excerpts are from *Inspector Hound Returns,* by Keveren.

1. Draw a sharp sign in each blue box to form the chromatic half steps ascending in the right-hand part. Play this excerpt.

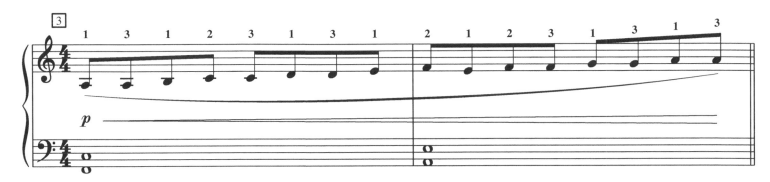

2. Draw a flat sign in each blue box below, to form the chromatic half steps descending in the left-hand part. Play this excerpt.

3. Write the correct scale fingering for the right hand in the blue boxes, then play this excerpt.

4. Play the three excerpts one after the other, without pausing, or add improvised measures and give this piece your own title. Descriptive words such as "sneaky," "eerie," and "mysterious" might give you some ideas.

Mysterious Patterns

Draw a line to connect each two-measure, mystery scale pattern in Column **A** to the key in Column **B** that will unlock it.

A   **B**

1.    C Major

2.    Chromatic

3.    D Major

4.    B Minor

5.    F Major

6.    B♭ Major

7.    G Minor

8.    A Minor

33

Use with Lesson Book 5, pg. 43

Haven't We Met Before?

Composers often use patterns, phrases, motives and sequences to unify a composition. Recognizing these elements in a piece provides a short-cut to secure learning.

The following excerpt is from *The Clown*, by Rebikov (measures 36-40).

1. The repetition of the same rhythms and intervallic patterns at a different pitch is called a _____.
2. In measures 37-39, block the notes of each half-measure. The first one has been circled and identified as a model. Circle each similar pattern, then play each one.
3. Identify the chord you circled by writing the letter symbol in the blue boxes.

A three-note motive is used throughout *Fantasia*, by Telemann.

1. In measures 1 and 3, the motive appears _____ times in the right-hand part.
2. In measure 1, the motive is repeated as a sequence beginning on what notes? _____, _____, and _____
3. Are measures 1 and 3 the same, or different? _____
4. The left-hand notes in measures 1 and 3 are identical. Which triad do they outline? _____

The following excerpt is from the *Menuet in G Minor*, in the "Notebook for Anna Magdalena Bach" (measures 9-16).

1. How long is the **question** phrase that begins in measure 9? _____ measures
2. How long is the **answer**? _____ measures
3. Is the **answer** parallel or contrasting? _____
4. What is the term for the repeated melodic pattern in measures 13 and 14? _____

The following excerpt is from *A Minor Contribution*, by Boyd (measures 8-13).

1. What are the first two intervals in the bass clef of measure 9? _____ and _____
2. How many times does that pattern of intervals appear in measures 9-12? _____
3. Does the left-hand move higher or lower? _____
4. The notes of the motive are circled in the treble clef. Name the interval between the first note and the last note inside the circle. _____
5. Circle the notes of each motive that follows. How many times does the sequence appear in measures 9-12? _____
6. Does it move higher or lower each time? _____

35

Use with Lesson Book 5, pg. 47

Thinking It Over

Match the chord name with its musical notation
by writing the correct number in each blank.

1. diminished triad

    a. _____

2. **iv** in D Minor

    b. _____

3. **iii** in B♭ Major

    c. _____

4. 2nd inversion chord

    d. _____

5. **ii** in D Major

    e. _____

6. open position chord

    f. _____

7. 1st inversion chord

    g. _____

8. **vi** in C Major

    h. _____

9. augmented triad

    i. _____

10. **V** in G Minor

    j. _____

Canon in D for Me

1. Play these open position chords in D Major.

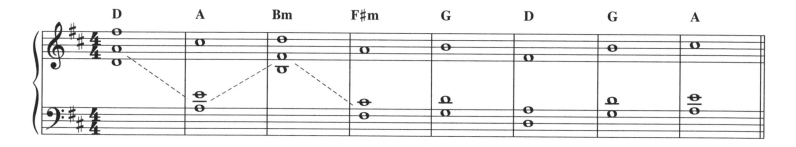

2. Play this chord progression that uses open position chords in D Major.

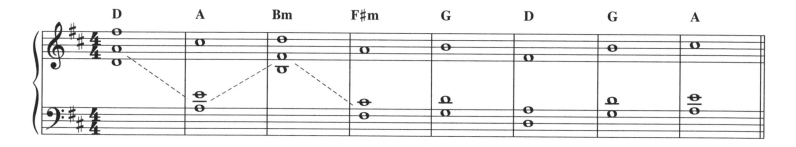

3. Continue the two-measure motive below as a sequence throughout this phrase. Write the melody using only notes from the D Major Scale. Notice that the first note of each sequence is the third of the chord in open position.

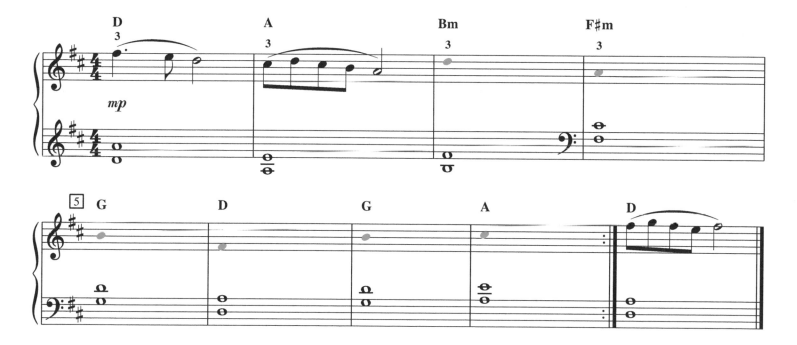

4. Create your own right-hand melody over the left-hand progression in the example above, using only notes from the D Major scale.

37

Use with Lesson Book 5, pgs. 48-50

Spike Is Puzzled

You and Spike are allowed to use your **Piano Lessons Book 5** to help find the answers to this musical crossword puzzle.

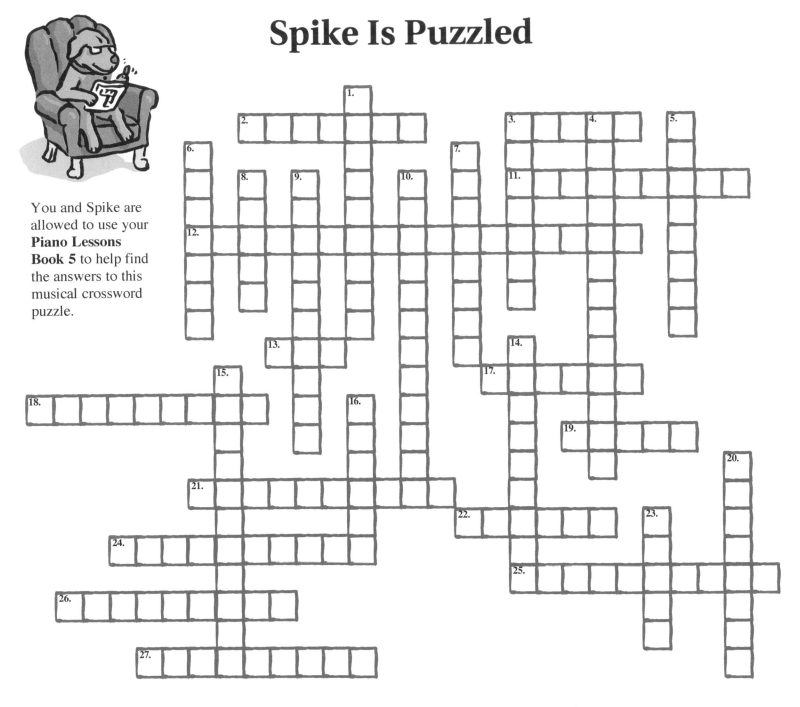

Across

2. "Dying," fading away
3. The highness or lowness of a tone
11. (with 23 Down) A triad built on the 2nd, 3rd, or 6th tone of any scale
12. A phrase that begins the same as a question, but varies the ending
13. The tonal center based on the tonic note of the scale
17. Suddenly
18. Little by little
19. Very
21. Broad *ritardando*
22. A short pattern of notes that reappears throughout a piece
24. Playfully
25. A minor triad with the 5th lowered one half-step
26. A sudden, strong accent
27. Moving by half-steps

Down

1. A chord in which the bass note is not the root
3. Heavily
4. Chord tones played as close together as possible, usually within an octave
5. Gracefully
6. Stressed, accented note
7. Lightly
8. A melody that is repeated exactly by a different voice
9. A smooth glide from one note to another
10. A triad built on the 1st, 4th, or 5th tone of any scale
14. A major triad with the 5th raised one half-step
15. Becoming faster
16. Play smooth and connected
20. Repetition of the same pattern of notes at a different pitch
23. (See 11 Across)

Answers on pg. 40

Teacher's Examples

Page 12 (Play)

Page 21 (Play)

Ode To Joy

1.

The Star Spangled Banner

2.

Simple Gifts

3.

Alouette

4.

Page 19 (Play)

B Natural Minor

1.

D Major

2.

F Major

3.

D Harmonic Minor

4.

B Harmonic Minor

5.

D Natural Minor

6.

Page 23 (Clap)

1.

2.

3.

4.

5.

Teacher's Examples - continued

Page 29 (Play)

Key of G Major

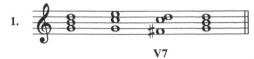

1.

V7

Key of F Major

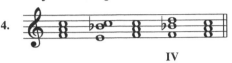

4.

IV

Key of D Major

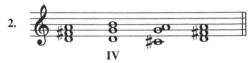

2.

IV

Key of B Minor

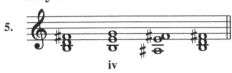

5.

iv

Key of C Minor

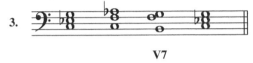

3.

V7

Key of E Minor

6.

i

Page 36 (Answers)

a.	4
b.	2
c.	5
d.	1
e.	3
f.	9
g.	7
h.	10
i.	8
j.	6

Page 38 (Answers)

Across

2. *Morendo*
3. Pitch
11. Secondary
12. Contrasting Answer
13. Key
17. *Subito*
18. *Poco a poco*
19. *Molto*
21. *Allargando*
22. Motive
24. *Scherzando*
25. Diminished
26. *Sforzando*
27. Chromatic

Down

1. Inversion
3. *Pesante*
4. Close Position
5. *Grazioso*
6. *Marcato*
7. *Leggiero*
8. Canon
9. *Portamento*
10. Primary Triad
14. Augmented
15. *Accelerando*
16. *Legato*
20. Sequence
23. Triad